THE WAR POEMS

To my grandfathers, who fought separate wars. One learned to live after WWI with a white fog of gas entrenched in his lungs. The other learned to live with a white feather delivered to the door he would walk through to Canada, where his eldest son would join the next war and die in a plane when it struck the ground.

THE WAR POEMS
Screaming at Heaven

by Keith Inman

Black Moss Press
2014

Copyright © 2014 Keith Inman

Inman, Keith, author
    The war poems : screaming at heaven / Keith Inman.

ISBN 978-0-88753-541-3 (pbk.)

1. War poetry. I. Title.

PS8617.N5438W27 2014   C811'.6   C2014-903741-4

Cover image by Seita, courtesy of Shutterstock
Design & Layout: Jason Rankin
Editor: Vanessa Shields

Published by Black Moss Press at 2450 Byng Road, Windsor, Ontario, N8W 3E8. Canada. Black Moss books are distributed in Canada and the U.S. by Fitzhenry & Whiteside. All orders should be directed there.
    Fitzhenry & Whiteside
    195 Allstate Parkway
    Markham, ON
    L3R 4T8

Black Moss Press (EST. 1969)

Black Moss would like to acknowledge the generous financial support from both the Canada Council for the Arts and the Ontario Arts Council.

ONTARIO ARTS COUNCIL / CONSEIL DES ARTS DE L'ONTARIO
50 YEARS OF ONTARIO GOVERNMENT SUPPORT OF THE ARTS
50 ANS DE SOUTIEN DU GOUVERNEMENT DE L'ONTARIO AUX ARTS

Canada Council for the Arts   Conseil des arts du Canada

Many of the poems in this book have been previously published, anthologized, placed in contests, or shared through the following publications: Descant, CV2, The Toronto Quarterly, Black Moss Press, Hidden Brook Press, Cubicle Press, Siligate Press, Cranberry Tree Press, The Saving Bannister, Hammered Out, Riveredge, PRECIPCe, robmclennansblogspot, Spring Pulse, Other Voices, Synapse Niagara, Amethyst Review, Ascent Aspirations, and VersaFire.

CONTENTS

WARS OF DEPENDENCE: 1812 TO 1887
Asylum	10
River Scout	11
A Measure of Powder	13
Bootlegging	14
The Whores Said	16
Darkness	18
Across the Father's Fields	19
She Who Sees Morning	21
Marta	22
Lars	23
Thresholds	24
At the Hunter's Table, They Ate Death	25
All Things	27
Time	28
In the Light of a Perfect Dawn	29
Hildie	30
Bridgette and François	31
Junjun	32
When Clouds Touch Down, A Year of Surrender	33
Albertha	34
Ms. R. E.	35

A REPUBLIC MONARCHY: 1889 TO 1953
Under the Sky's Fire	38
The Flute and the Rifle	39
Mining Souls	40
Fukyeusal	41
Cold Water Feed	43
Blue Chagall	45
Two Jesus Ways	46
Grace	47
Aromatic Wood	49
When Tomorrow Comes	51
Johnny	52
Joe's Place	53
'Pon The Mall	54
(B)rush Stroke	56
A Restoration Fable	57

Margery	58
Design	59
A Parish Swan	60
Refrigeration Class	61
Barbed Wire and Wild Roses	62
Jerry	63
Soldier's Heart	65
Teem	67
Smelting	68

ARMED PEACE: 1954 TO PRESENT

Dargmar and Jorge	70
How Soft the Snow	71
Handful of Wind	72
Trigger	73
Summer of 65	75
Always, There Are Flowers	76
Home Reno	78
Faith	79
Old My Guitar	80
Dutchie	82
I of Death	83
Susie	84
Randy	85
The Blue Charger	87
Ms. N	89
Nan's Mom	91
Greg: Corp of Engineers, Afghanistan	93
Maeve	94
Dwayne	95
To Sail Gracefully	96
Demo	97
Over the Field, A Lark Flutters - Rememberance Day	99

Acknowledgements	103
About the Author	103

People rely on reason to form and inform their lives. But what happens when time and circumstance get in the way? And what then is reason?

WARS OF DEPENDENCE: 1812 TO 1887

" to stare back down
the dark hallway of a moment ago

Chris Banks

ASYLUM

1812: Napoleon's army defeats Russia, 20,000 of 5,000,000 men survive; Brothers Grimm publish Fairy Tales; *America serves papers for Canada to surrender; opposing Generals from each country agree to have dinner the following month, after the war is finished*

Leon chewed slowly
his jaw jutting slightly as he mushed
the re-heated mash against the roof of his mouth.

George cracked heart-nuts
from the glass dish
on the table.

He'd told his ma
he was joining the Green Tigers.
Told her
about Asylum
for Leon.

Leon smiled,
a thin crooked wedge in a face
half opened with sunlight late for rising,
when he heard his name.
He patted George on the shoulder
as their mother hobbled with a cane
scraped the remains of her dinner
into the bucket for the pig. "I want
neither of you to go," she said,
stooped at the basin. "Is that
being selfish."

George had to grab his tea
to rinse the nut paste
from his throat.

Leon held his plate out for more.

RIVER SCOUT

1812: Abu Simbel discovered by Europeans; Red River, Manitoba, founded; Books in circulation: Cuvier's research on fossils, Avogadro's molecular composition of gases, Maclure's observations on geology

It was warm for Spring. The rivers
raced with run-off. And, the horses
were nervous. William led them
down a winding curve of the escarpment's
limestone gravity of hammered stratii.

He was to meet Brock for supper,
and face the eventual argument on
continental shift, and whose fault that was.
All William knew
was that the earth had endured more
catastrophe than all the cracked tea cups
in China, and India for that matter.

They rode on along one of the many
small cataracts that channeled
the peninsula into miled sections
A dense fog ceilinged the lower
fields of stubbled-grass and orchards.

Beyond hedgerows and side lanes,
oil lamps from sheds and houses
shone upward in narrow shafts, holding
the evenings canvas in place
as a sword of the moon sheened fearward
from the fortress pines to the Southeast.

They rode quickly, picking up speed,
until the horses suddenly reared
at an oxbow corner to the river. Toads
covered the path; were being squashed
under the horses hooves. Didn't
they know about crossed lines?

The men dismounted onto the slippery mass;
they sniffed for ambush. Silence
drifted from the embanked marsh.
The horses stamped. On this cricket-less night,
wet hides thumped their pillared legs.

A MEASURE OF POWDER

1813: Turner paints Frosty Morning; *Bolivar becomes dictator of Venezuela; Mexico declares independence; Jane Austen publishes* Pride and Prejudice; *McGill is founded; the waltz conquers Europe; war in the Canadas turns vicious*

The earth exploded.
Her ears rang. An obtuse light
fractured the room. The kitchen.
She was in the kitchen. Her feet
on the smashed table. Head
on the boards. The roof tilted
at an odd angle. She stumbled
through the door. Men screamed. Fire
lit her face. "What in he…" The
wall was a tumbled mash
of timber, a torso and a Private's
hat. Blood drained
onto the steaming ground.
She ran across the courtyard.
Grape shot crackled. Smoke rose
from the south rise. Shrill voices
echoed between buildings.
A Captain grabbed her arm.
"There's been four direct hits. Ma'am,
please, take yourself to the infirmary."
"The magazine's on fire!"
"Are you positive, Ma'am?"
"Measure your shot, young sir!"
"Aid the infirm, ma'am." The boy
saluted and turned toward the smoke.
The infirmary door stood ajar.
Something soft, like a pile of clothes,
blocked it. She pushed hard,
and the pooling darkness revealed itself
in its bloodied white shift.

BOOTLEGGING

1813: Verdi and Wagner are born; Americans burn York (Toronto) and Fort George (Newark), reoccupy Detroit; Shelley publishes Queen Mab; *Techumseh dies in battle; Brits and Canadians light up Youngston and Buffalo*

Arms crossed against any whisper
of heat that scorched the corners
of Lillian's dark porch —
racing flames had chased
the narrow town lanes
for sleeping Rangers who'd re-christened
Yankees with terror —
Newark smoldered
in the wreckage of dawn.

And the Bootlegger's shack on the far
corner, an ash heap drowned
into ditches. The silent ambulance
of haloed horses steamed the air
with their breath.

Her steady stream of letters
poured into the wormed framework
of city hall; those
logger-headed men,
tasting her final straw
to their fiery existence. Though
they'd pop up anew,
days later, a month at most,
beyond some quilted huddle of farms.

Town folks picked through charred
timbers, their faces filled with shadows
of misfortune and silent prayer
for the dead.
And why, for heavens sake,
did their warring cousins
from across the river burn
a Bootlegger's on the other side of town?

Lillian rubbed lavender in her hands
and up her arms. She drew the curtains
and held her bible tight
against the flames that licked her rafters.

THE WHORES SAID

1814-5:Washington is set afire; Madison flees, Molly stays, hides the silver; Pope Pius VII resumes the Inquisition; Goya paints Third of May; *Wellington and Blucher defeat Napoleon; David Riccardo writes on the low price of corn and how it can affect the stock market*

Gilly had learned about flight from the roof
of the livery, watching British Regulars
parade their paces when his American cousin,
Abraham, started whistling stones
at his head. One grazed his shoulder and he
mis-stepped; bounced a foot in the dust.
Madam Lucielle called him Gilly with a limp.
He ended up in the ir-regulars learning
how to 'stick' a sack of sedge, the townfolk
called him Gimpy. In the summer of '13,

Abe returned talking about a Chesapeake
boarding and Fulton's 'Nautilus' sub-
marinin' any Brit-ship, "You jus' watch us."
And he jabbered on that ole Nap-o-lin
would never rule the world. Gilly's
third cousin, Holly, from upstate,
came too, coy and fair, all ribboned
and bowed in a New England flair.

Gil flew south into a new militia. A political
Captain, and his wall of other men's trophies,
had a plan for Gil, and the re-making
of Newark. But he wasn't so lucky burning
his old home town, as the invaders re-
formed at the river. Some stray shot
tore his spine something good. Left him
with a double limp. By '14, Holly
had flown toward fortunes in Quebec
and New Brunswick trade. The Neutrals helped Gil
flee across a bridge of buckled ice.

Back on the Upper in '15, the only place that'd
serve him were the Whores, who'd watched
their Fort flare, and munitions red-rocket
glare through a Newark night. But,
a whole new line of capital had flooded in.
He's a bit splintered of his own authority now,
throwin' his glass every then and again,
saying he likes the way light flies.

DARKNESS

1816: Byron publishes The Siege of Corinth, Coleridge *pens* Kubla Khan; *Brewster invents the kaleidoscope; American Bible Society founded; Scots and French fight over furs*

Theo was in for trading pelts
from the wrong Indians through
the wrong Company to the wrong
nation. The One-Who-Looks-At-Midnight
had knifed a killer, a thief and a rapist.
"They in here, too?" Theo asked,
handing Midnight a flask
as they walked 'the yard' away
from sentries. Midnight
didn't wonder how a man got whiskey
into jail. He knew colour could decide
fate, among other things, the way birch
could take over a forest of pine, only
trees allow others time to reseed.

Midnight passed the flask
as they turned a corner. "One man.
He live in ground now talking to sky.
Judge say I must be full of shame."
Midnight smiled a small crest of moon, smoke
clouded from his cragged face
turning back to stone.

They sat sleepy-eyed in the common
cell across from Arly the bootlegger,
and Jacques the fighter. Outside
the iron bolt lock, the inside guard
kept an eye to the split board door.

Midnight sang a story of searching
for game giving itself up
to feed the people, and of hiding
from the white of the moon. Later,
they hung Riel.

ACROSS THE FATHER'S FIELDS

1835: Hans Christian Anderson publishes his first children's tales; battery powered trains begin; P.T. Barnum opens an exhibition; Victor Cousin's phrase 'Art for Art's Sake' comes into use; an Irish Miller burns out his French rivals in Bytown (Ottawa), starts a 10 year war

Just north of where fields got raided
and barns burned, Lil' Jim was gonna get it
for doing and lying about what he said he didn't.
Big Jim unlooped his belt, and whooped
his boy real good, then told him how
at his age he'd removed old man Shaw's
front step, banged on the door nine times
and ran like Hell. "Got a shit kickin'
from the old man. Had to plough and tend
Shaw's crops all summer while Shaw
milked the cow. You best keep runnin'
boy, 'cause I can not help you this time."
Lil' Jim looked over the creek valley back
of the barns still standing along Concession
26 where the sun was rising like torches
that had come bobbing down the hill,
straight for him, framing him in the bright
cones of the cedar alcove he was hiding
in, like someone knew he was there. And
Harry Kronin yelling his name, calling him
a thief, barking it like a yappy dog, 'cause
Harry's short, and don't come off so
tough. But he'd iron in his hand, laid it
up against Lil' Jim's cheek, the steel
shivering the skin. And yet, Lil' Jim
went and said, "What horses, Mr. Kronin,"
just as they snorted down along the ravine.
And Harry turned to the others and said,
"There's a much bigger problem here."
And with another Kronin holding rope,
Lil' Jim twisted away and grabbed a sharp
rock, whipped it at the brother, but missed,
smashing younger Harry's eye like a broken
egg. Old Harry moon-dogged as Lil' Jim

ran like hounds were nipping his heels.
All through the rutted night fields, and stone-
filled creeks, willow branches, spiders,
and buzzing mosquitoes he sweat, and swore,
wearing the biggest grin you ever saw, till morning.

SHE WHO SEES MORNING

1837:Victoria's reign begins; Morse exhibits his telegraph in NewYork; Canadians fight for reform, their troops sink the USS Caroline ferrying insurgents across the Niagara River

The season was dry

a winter without snow

the ground, a gnarled
deer-brown tinged
with frozen patches of grass,
neither rich
nor absent of hope.

She laid back down.

His weight pressed against her,
the rough cheek scratching her shoulder.

He didn't wake,

a thick hide bundled
in his arms
the way words stayed
under his tongue —

the skins pulled from her breast
as morning climbed over.

MARTA

1838: Oliver Twist *and* Nicholas Nickleby *are best sellers;* The Great Western *steams the Atlantic under 15 days; Canada is a Monarchy or a Republic; insurgents raid the border*

Put the wooden horse away so the other boy can play.
Nnnnooooo.
Look at the cow. You like cows.
Nnnnooooo.
Put the horse back?
Nnnooowwwaaahhh!
Okay!

-

Let the little boy play.

-

Let him play.

-

Give it to him.

-

Give it.
Nnnnooooo.
The horse is dirty.

-

It's dirty.

-

Give it.
Nnnnooooo.
Wanna grape?

-

Put the horse in the toy box.

-

There we go. Nice. Give it nice.

-

Here we go.
Nnnnooooo.
How about THIS toy?

-

Look at this one! It makes a noise.
mmmmmnnnnnooooo.
Share the toy with the little boy?
NO!

LARS

1858-9: Darwin publishes On the Origin of Species; *Victoria declares Ottawa, a city between two of her warring people, their capital; gold found in Fraser Canyon; Blondin crosses the Niagara River; war between Canada and U.S. averted over a dead pig*

You wouldn't catch Lars out there
against this wind.
Not on days when the forest
flew around into tumbled,
broken lean-tos.

He laid his palm against the glass,
felt the pulse
of wind bending trees
into the river
behind the cabin. Let the current
carry away the fallen,
he'd walk the banks next
clear day, chop out the dammed
that would flood his hectares
beyond the evergreens,
his woven wall against the north
that furled the river's face into a grim,
fall frown. The path

beyond the cedar fence,
to the next Homesteader, the one
with steeples on each peak pointing
to angry clouds, was obscured
by wild grass, the owner,
starved out before thirty,
third along the Concessions to do so.

By the tall elm, a mass
of leaves swirled up into a small cyclone
as tall as a man. It walked
to the edge then stepped off
onto the steady pull from shore
and crossed the constant push
against rock.

THRESHOLDS

1861-2:American Civil War begins; 50,000 Cdns will enlist; R. J. Gatling builds a gun; Dostoevsky publishes House of the Dead, *Victor Hugo,* Les Miserables; *while Pasteur theorizes on germ fermentation, Henry David Thoreau dies of complications from a cold*

The letter in the news was a worn story
like the paper would become

two months a war vet writing to his mother about his best friend shot
through the ears beside him. "We were jus' talking." "Don't tell
his ma." "Ma," the letter ended, "pray for me." Will told his
sister beside him at breakfast that he knew this soldier,
that he'd worked at the mill. A miserable ole rumple
of blue cotton driving a tumbril all day. The coot
complained about his back bouncing
across thresholds of stone, until
he and his brother inherited
land. It seemed like a
fortune.
Up and quit right then
and there. Moved out west. Left
his wife and kids in a little house in
Merry Town. Will knew the girl, went out
with her for a bit. A real doll with a pouffed
helmet of starched hair, full drink of blood red
lips, church-window nails, bayonet lashes rarely
blinking over cannon eyes and pinched pink rosettes
of bright red cheeks below dark-arch brows afraid to be touched.
And Will, a wind-blown seed rooted in rock, sprouting, ready to unroll.

They say the land was a parched stretch
of debt when war began.

AT THE HUNTER'S TABLE, THEY ATE DEATH

1863: B.C. natives see their first guns, one tribe destroys another; T. H. Huxley publishes Man's Place in Nature, *J. S. Mills,* Utilitarianism; Travel Insurance *is available in Hartford, Connecticut*

"So we can live," the Hunter laughed.
But, the repast was heavy. The Journalist
broke from the gorge and leaned back,
looked through the sheer curtains
to catch a glimpse of the forest.
It was nearly sunset.
The tops of the trees were aflame
as vultures circled in the mauve light.

This man's property was a barbed lot, wired
hectares of trees, known as a bush, nothing more.
However, earlier that day, when they strolled the grounds,
the Hunter felt at ease, saying, "The forest
is the country of my heart; its deep
layered interior full of evergreens
arrowing upward, harvesting the sun. And geese,
look at them, there, flying in formation
searching the most tenderest shoots."

He scoured the heavens, as they walked,
then suddenly raised his arm and bullets
exploded into sky. Branches
and geese were torn from the clouds,
out-stretched wings tumbled like crosses.
The Journalist's fist clenched. But a hand
fell on his shoulder. The Hunter whispered,
"Stick your head in the ground, if you're so
indignant. Roots strangle their rivals.
Or watch the geese across the river
consume an entire years crop. Is that
who you rage for?"

The food God provided was praised.
They'd eaten heartily, boisterously, and the host
offered more wine, or a shot of liqueur.

In the window the evening fluttered,
all the bright colours having slipped into darkness
as the writer drank his solemn dram.

ALL THINGS

1864-5: Cheyenne and Arapahoe massacred at Sand Creek; Lincoln assassinated; Tolstoi finishes War and Peace, *Lewis Carroll,* Alice in Wonderland; *Canadian E.P. Doherty hunts down John Wilkes Booth*

The sun was warm. James
undid his jacket, but kept
walking against the brisk
wind, a satchel of sugar
and flour cutting his hand.
He switched sides and blood
flushed through his fingers.

A crowd at the church across
the field flowed onto the hard,
winter grass under a bare tree.
A hearse pulled away
down the long lane, shining
under sun-fused branches
receiving the dead. A woman,

her face a cloud, stood
in the mud, pouring cold
rain into another's heart,
an arm wrapped around her
shoulders. James turned down
his own street. Over the lake
a deep, blue pall of sky

had stalled. He walked toward
its bellyful of snow touching the earth.
At home, he pondered the work
of God as the log fire popped
and hissed — water to vapour,
solid to spirit, mass
to energy — the measure of matters.

TIME

1866: Greeks revolt against Turks; Friedrich Lange publishes History of Materialism; *Degas begins his ballet scenes;* Fenians bring their war to Canada; American Congress raises questions about Canada funding Booth and his cohorts

under the bar lamps
was one long guzzle
of memories.

You
tilting back glasses
of golden elixir, washing down
the face that loomed
in the mirrored shelves;

that night,
fumbling for keys lost
in the glare of the polished bar, conversation
tight in your throat,
a sentence for one.

Words slurred
across empty stools,
you counted foam rings
around the glass.

Then it was time to go, you said,
into the night, staggering
down the dark dancing tracks
where they say, a candle
came to meet you.

IN THE LIGHT OF A PERFECT DAWN

1867: Diamonds discovered in S. Africa; Cezanne paints Rape; *Canada forms a Government to check & balance against U.S. style democracy, create a Dominion of Peace, Order & Good Government; Ouida publishes* Under Two Flags

Morning spilled
across the horizon,

striking the trees
down with light.

Shadows lengthened,
then fled back east.

HILDIE

1869: Red River Rebellion erupts; Matthew Arnold writes on culture and anarchy; First Vatican Council discusses Papal infallibility; J.S. Mills publishes On the Subjection of Women; *critics argue over what the women represent in Manet's* Balcony *painting*

Her big flowered hat
keeps out the sun
as mauve leather gloves
keep out the dirt,
but not infernal weeds
from rooting the grass.

Robins
scratch at worms. She
pulls the earth,
picks blackberries
plants tomatoes, herbs
pole beans and Scotch

Bloom. By afternoon,
a granddaughter learns to kick
a swirling blue ball and not
pick dandelions with bees on them

as a son-in-law talks about
changing the world
one vote at a time.
He doesn't mean women
and has no idea how to stop a war,
but can barbecue
a mean rack of ribs over an

open fire.
She works
at these moments
that pass.

BRIDGETTE AND FRANÇOIS

1870-1: Prussia lays siege to Paris; Italians march on Rome; Jules Verne publishes Twenty Thousand Leagues Under the Sea; *Heinrich Schliemann excavates Troy; Wagner marries Lizst's daughter; Paul Kane dies aged 60 after his daily walk*

They arrived home from the funeral.
Bridgette carrying memories of her father
the way he'd carried her
after scraping her knee. Or,
those beard scratching Christmas
kisses from a poorly disguised Saint
Nickolaus. The shrinking
bundle of bones
shuffling along the hard echo
of the back hall, nothing
other than passing could resolve.

After steadying the horse
for the night, Françios found her standing
in the doorway to the kitchen,
hands twelved at her mouth.
Her father's clock on the floor.

He took her wrists
and pulled their stiffness gently
to her sides, stilted her
to the couch, poured
a crystal of brandy and talked

soft ideas of tomorrow's light
for her to sleep through
midnight's long, drawn out

hours. By morning
he had the hole patched,
limed and sanded.
The wall smooth, retouched. Time
hung for dinner in its cracked
case on a new nail. The rewinding key
deep inside.

JUNJUN

1873: Financial panic in New York; James Clerk Maxwell publishes Electricity and Magnetism; *Rimsky-Korsakov's* Ivan the Terrible *opens in St. Petersburg; Remington gunworks produce their first typewriter*

Mrs. MacElwray was over for a visit
"Jus' wanted to catch up," she said
glancing around the cabin.

Junjun made a pot of English tea
and got out
the supply biscuits while
Mrs. MacElwray, who the neighbourhood
kids called - Mrs. Mackerel, spouted on
about her own Colleen having "the wastin'
disease. Can't do a thing, poor thing,
and Robert with the lump
in his head, which of course, is what
your oldest boy jus' died of. But, Sissy's
doing best. But that consumption, eh?
There's jus' so many with it
goin' round."

Junjun drank her tea down
to the dead leaves, a silent
waterfall from a delicate cup.

Just then her youngest came in with a large
axe over his shoulder.
He filled the doorway
his brown skin covered in sweat, saying
his 'How to do's' to the startled
Mrs. Fishlady.

"Damn old stump, ma. Jus'
a buried gnarl of old roots
that won't break down.
You okay, Mrs. Mackerel?"

WHEN CLOUDS TOUCH DOWN, A YEAR OF SURRENDER

1885: Charles Dickens' son, Garrison Commandeer Francis Dickens, capitulates to Big Bear; Riel and Poundmaker surrender to the British, Big Bear to Sam Steele; Gordon killed in Khartoum: the Mahati dies; Galton proves individuality of fingerprints; Riel is hanged

It rained the day Seamus went in
and when he walked from under
the high-spiked Jack flying
over the block. His father

pulled up in a Tumbril cart,
and they rattled off. Their words
locked in their fists;
too many potholes
in the road already.

A Coach passed,
heading toward the shops.
A red-haired lady glanced down
and away. Her top-hatted husband
folded his paper, stared
at Seamus, then,
the road they'd travelled.
Seamus wondered
if he'd be checking for his wallet
in a moment.

Lightning flashed over the lake.
Thunder rattled his bones.
"Look at me when I talk to you, lad.
Your Uncle's got you free. You're to join
your brothers, now."

Along the King's Road,
clouds touched down.

ALBERTHA

1886: Canadian Pacific Railway is completed; Hydroelectric installations begin in Niagara Falls; last Impressionist exhibit in Paris; R. L. Stevenson publishes Dr. Jekyll and Mr. Hyde.

Albertha liked her second beer
better than the first.

Liked to watch
from the corner table
beside the bottled glass, as the sun
crossed the bar.

She kept her hat on,
upturned flower pot
covering silver turned-up curls.

Greeted everyone with a hello,
a smile, a scowl, or guffaw,
depending on the depth of her beer.

And when the ambulance horses
raced up the street,
"Is it Art?
Have they come for old Art?"

She saw the torches
dance past, decided
to stay for a few more
before heading back
across the tracks.

She must have stood waiting
just down the lane-way, where the saw mill
met the dump at the crossing
before the after-dinner train
shuffled along under the beamed bridge,
box cars swaying, re-balancing themselves
on rails that climbed the autumn hills
       into clouds that lay flat
              against an evening sky.

MS. R. E.

1887: Arthur Conan Doyle writes his first Sherlock Holmes story, A Study in Scarlet; *Verdi's opera* Otello *opens in Milan, Gilbert and Sullivan's* Ruddigore *in London; within a year Jack the Ripper preys on London women*

In church, the old maid sat prim
in her pew whispering forward
that her sister's boy, young Mr. E.,
would kill all the rats in the tenant
farms down the road. The preacher
below the cross of the congregation
touched his chest, then his brow, pulled
stone anecdotes from his mind's eye
and hurled them through a pointed finger.
They hit the restless like rough agates
that bounced away to roll in the seams
of the wooden floor and lay hidden
in dark shadows below leaded glass.

After the sermon, he stood outside
the oak door, "It'd be a godsend
to get rid of them," he told Ms R. E.
and shook hands with her neighbours.
The kids took off leaving behind their
Sunday shine and ran down the alley.

They found Mr. E. leaning on a heart-
shaped shovel along side the homes,
rags stuffed in low tunneling burrows,
the smell of whale oil everywhere,
and a pipe lit dangling from his lip.
His white shirt and oiled boots
were spattered with mud and blood.
At his feet, a small pile of bone
laced fur twisted with tails
and studded with black jeweled eyes
reflected in a pool of sky. Mr. E.
glared at the kids with his 'got 'em all'
stare. But that night the children
heard scratching in the wood pile
and threw rocks at fiery eyes.

A REPUBLIC MONARCHY:
1889 TO 1953

> transparent as shadows they labour
> in their manufacture of light
>
> Al Purdy

UNDER THE SKY'S FIRE

1899: British Empire goes to war against Boers; Ibsen writes When We Dead Awaken, *Oscar Wilde,* The Importance of Being Earnest, *Alexander Bain,* The Realization of the Possible; *first magnetic sounds are recorded; French pointillist Alfred Sisley dies*

Danny walks
with his father as they plough
the field. "I want you
with me, son," he'd said
at breakfast.

They work now
without words, hats
askew, cotton shirts
billowing
in the unwavering sun.

A wheeling kite of crows
and gulls rise
and dive behind them, horses
driving ahead of the brown
ground folding over

the salt from Danny's brow
hissing on the flat unturned earth
before the blade.

THE FLUTE AND THE RIFLE

1900: Boxer rising in China; Fenians bomb Welland Canal; Sigmund Freud publishes The Interpretation of Dreams; *first Browning Revolver manufactured; Cezanne paints* Still Life with Onions; *Reginald Fressenden transmits his voice over radio waves; Puccini's* Tosca *opens*

They sang to us
on the farms, those
men of government
and their language of sticks
and stones
so that we'd know
the story.

Epiphany came later

a book slammed shut,
the sharp breath of bullets
whistling through the soft reeds
of our beliefs

and we fell

to the creeks
and blowing grass
of hillsides riddled red
with flowers
blooming from the bones
we planted.

MINING SOULS

1901: Boers turn to guerrilla warfare; Cuba falls under U.S. protection; B. S. Roundtree authors Poverty, A Study of Town Life; *Walt Disney is born; world turns its back on steam, the age of electricity begins*

The white sun
along a far reach of cliff,

broken away
into western seas,

bleaches the leached ore
into bright days for tomorrow.

Yet this ordinate star, this sol ordained,
can not, and will never, teach

the coppery core
to change colour.

FUKYEUSAL

1902: Boers sign for peace; Orange Free State becomes British; Trotsky escapes from Siberian prison; Andre Gide publishes The Immoralist, *J. A. Hobson* Imperialism; *Oliver Heaviside finds an atmospheric layer which aids the conduction of radio waves*

They hated 'The Bruce' to a man,
not because he was crazy
not because he was lazy
but because he called them both
crazy bastards and lazy mothers.
"Yeusless bunch, yeus. Fukyeusal.
Yeu donna wha wark is," he'd laugh,
his eyes narrowed over the spiked mug
welded to his thick hand
as they hammer-wedged a gear, tall as a man,
out from the finger-crushing-mesh
of an idled
newspaper machine.

"Yeu need a hand do ya? Weel call yer mamma, boy.
Now, Fukyeus, an git that thing aout!"

Metal bars pried
between steam lines feeding dryers
hot as a sun; skin
branded by sizzling
touch. McAlester
saying "Therre's narr a trruce in 'The Brruce,'"
jumped the fence at lunch
caught a hundred grasshoppers in a jar,
left it in the office of 'The Bruce,'
lid off.

His last day came a month
before retirement, dropping
an old water tower. The welder
called "Clear!" before cutting the last
leg. 'The Old Bruce' couldn't stand
the air hose left coiled like a snake
under the steel/oak drop
and stole-in to save
the companies rubber as two ton
let go. The curve
of tank caught him
from behind, rolled his knee up past
his head, his eyes squeezed out as he hissed,
"Fffuuukkkyyyeeeeuuusssaaalll…"

COLD WATER FEED

1914: Austrian Archduke Francis Ferdinand assassinated; Austria declares war on Serbia; Germany on Russian, France and Belgium; Britain on Germany; Austria on Russia; Serbia on Germany; France on Austria; Austria on Belgium; Russia on Turkey…; James Joyce publishes The Dubliners; *Matisse unveils* The Red Studio; *Irving Berlin releases* Watch Your Step

Below the level of decay and pale
spidering roots, Harry heaved the wet
hemp rope around the bell of the pipe
as Farley handed Jonas another bucket of muck
from the collapsed earth that'd froze

real good last night to a thin-skinned,
undercut ice-pond of a sinkhole magnet
for the child's prying toe taking a shortcut
through the Machine Works to school.

Harry's foot squished deeper into the brackish
water an inch from the rim of his oiled boot.
"Pour the lead to 'er." Grey snakes slithered
off the rusted shell, sank out of sight.
Farley fumbled to loosen the forming sleeve
as a clump of far-wall slid into the trench,
flooding Harry's boot. Harry grabbed the bucket
and tossed the soupy mess over his shoulder.
A child's toque sloshed onto the grass.
Dark spots splattered the manager's suit.
"Keep it going, boys. Lines are down."

Jonas unclogged the pump-line in the back
of the Conestoga, and began cranking
again, straining under the weight of the body
of water being lifted from the pit.
Farley knocked a packing iron
off the hub. "Short a pair now."

"Is that cinder against the pipe? There!"
The engineer, in a skewed flapped cap
and glasses, pointed down from his Buckboard,
his muffled mitt demanding Farley toss
a raw handful up for him to breathe on. "Yep!"
The engineer squinted at the sky.
"Right under the hydro wire. Electrolysis!"
he exclaimed, as a cause of death.

BLUE CHAGALL

1915: Britain bombed from balloon ships; Germans use poison gas on Allies who hold their ground; Edgar Lee Masters publishes Spoon River; *Ford produces his millionth car; Margaret Sangster jailed for writing on birth control; Einstein talks about Relativity*

Waiting for the answer
from God, the goat
picks up a fiddle.

TWO JESUS WAYS

1916: A day after battle, 68 of 753 members of the Newfoundland Regiment answer roll call; Vicente Blasco Ibanez writes The Four Horsemen of the Apocalypse; *Jazz sweeps the States; Blood refrigerated for later use; Tommy gun invented; Rasputin murdered*

If I could
go back and do it again
what would I gain, eh.

If I could leap them there stars
so high and far.
But how would I start.

Would I sing,
a song of common ling-o.
If I could wing it. I would.

Or hows 'bout I dance.
A few drunken steps of prancin', eh?
I'd take the chance for you, there, darlin'.

And I'd do it! For you.
'Cause I know how you're blue, all the time
over things like that when they're due.

And I'd do it for me, too, you know.
That's just the way I sees it.
And there ain't no two Jesus ways 'bout it.

GRACE

1917: U.S. declares war; 35,000 Americans had already joined Canadian Exposition Forces; Mata Hari executed as spy; Germans starve; T. S. Eliot publishes Prufrock; *Charlie Chaplin's salary reaches a million a year; Halifax, Nova Scotia, leveled by boat blast*

She shuffled along worn cement,
pocked and broken, under a beige
haze of sky. Stepped

up the brown, paint-peeled
veranda; market-bags stretched longer
than arms could lift. She

leaned against the door, waiting
for the humidity
to release its lock on the wood.

Clicked the radio on
in the kitchen
to the war report,
"over by Christmas. And now..." The shelves

she coloured
with packets of rations,
then the power went out   again.

The house slid
into heat. She reached along the picture-less hall
the way you'd reach through fog, found
the body of her bed.

A towel over the window,
a damp cloth haloed
her brow.

The fan on the vanity was silent,
its wide cross of blades unmoving
in the dusty mirror as the breathless
day pressed down, the static
buzz of cicadas singing
of death marching
toward an obscured sun.

AROMATIC WOOD

1918: at the 11th hour on the 11th day of the 11th month war to end war is ratified into peace; over a million have died; Spanish Flu kills 50 million; Rulers are assassinated, voted out, resign, abdicate; British women get the vote; a group of artists in Toronto meet to form the Algonquin School

Right after Granddad got really sick
a few family members asked for violins.
He answered plainly,
"You didn't want to play them.
You don't get them."
And he sold everything:
key, stock and string.
One of the last going to Dr. Sabley,
who could at least make it yowl.
Granddad's smile twisted as the doctor played.
Told him, "It's yours, no charge."
Uncle Jim was outraged.

But before young Sabley left with his prize,
Granddad stepped into the living room
raised the bow, and sawed chords.
Big Jim jumped from the easy chair.
"You still can't play," he yelled, snapping
his paper shut, and stormed out of the house,
his pipe puffing like a smouldering saxophone.

Granddad bid the doctor goodbye
and shuffled back down the hall.
He stopped to ruffle my hair,
"We live small lives," he said,
before returning to his straight-back chair.

Various stages of violins, vined
to the ceiling with string, were all
put in boxes as the venetian blind
cast a stairway shadow over the brushes,
pots of gel, glues, the old man's
angelic hair, the half-crook'd glasses.

Aromatic wood, like forest resin,
hung to his stained, white apron
as he cradled the last violin in his thin lap.
Tap, tap, pluck, plunk.

A dilapidated truck with wood-frame rails
drove up, a man, looked like an old buzzard,
shook hands with Granddad,
who loaded the boxes into the back;
across the street in the park, children screamed
and yelled, playing on the whirling merry-go-round;
Granddad stopped a moment, lifted the instrument
from its long box and aligned it in the sun –
light glistening along the carved, polished body,
a resounding sweep rose and curved upward
over the neighbourhood in a myriad of voices
calling from across an ocean where a soft blue wind
carried the fog of the past over the tops of the trees
before trembling again into silence

the old rusted truck drove away in a puff of blue smoke.
"Gone with the devil," Uncle Jim said, reclining on the porch.

WHEN TOMORROW COMES

1936: Hitler gets 99% of the vote; Spain erupts in war; Margaret Mitchell's Gone With the Wind *is published; Top films:* Modern Times *and* The Great Ziegfeld; *J. A. Mollison flies from Newfoundland to London in 13 hours 17 minutes*

How little we knew of homes
made of stone,
catching snakes by the tail.

They'd try and coil
up our arms but we'd
snap 'em,
break their backs.

How little we knew
climbing fences. Sharp
points of steel tearing
the seat of our pants.

We'd hide in the vines
until the farmer passed.
His flat-bed car
kicking up dust, pepper gun

at his side. How little
we knew shoving grapes
in our mouths,
a sweet tang like salt
on the tongue.

We filled our pockets,
'Don't look back,' we'd said
and ran. How little

we knew
the sound of a gun,
of crows scattering,
of an echoing sky.

JOHNNY

1937: Wall St heads toward recession; Ernest Hemingway writes To Have and Have Not; *Franco destroys Guernica, Picasso creates one; Popular songs:* Whistle While You Work, A Foggy Day In London Town; *Amelia Earhart lost; Hindenberg explodes at Lakehurst*

Johnny's wrench-scarred fingers
couldn't quite get at the tiny solenoid
that would fix the light atop his Ma's stove.

"The burners work okay," he said,
brushing aside his father's shaking
hammer-hands, as the once commanding voice
quavered, "Is the fuse fried!"

Johnny repeated loudly, "No. Another day!"
They'd already fixed the taps, the toilet, the bulb
at the head of the stairs.
They had tea instead.

Tying up his boots
on the back stairs,
his mother tried to fold a few dollars
into his pocket.
He waved it away.

She stood above him
on the landing, shades
of grey leaned on an arthritic hip.
"You're still my son.
I just want to help
until you find a job."

He opened the door to a blast of cold.
"I don't charge for labour, Ma."

JOE'S PLACE

1938: Japan invades China; Hitler appoints himself War Minister; Kristallnacht in Germany; Stuart Chase pens The Tyranny of Words, *William Faulkner* The Unvanquished; *Grote Reber picks up radio waves from the Milky Way; Orsen Wells broadcasts* War of the Worlds

When you first looked at the window
it was clean see-through
to the kitchen out back
as you drove by waving to Joe.

Later, you noticed
a cracked pane,
bubbles molded in the glass
paint peeling from wood
whose joints, loose and opening,
framed the pot-bellied man, leaning
forward in his straight-backed chair
at his great-grandfather's table,
soup-pot blister in the middle.

He'd sat there every night,
muscle-shirted, watching
the tide go in and out
a little later each day
until the midnight low
drained the dark way down.

'PON THEMALL

1939: Germany invades Poland; Second war to end war begins; U.S. declares neutrality over voter sentiment; The Wizard of Oz *loses the Academy Award; passenger liner Athenia bound for Montreal torpedoed by U-boat off Ireland*

War was a rumour
threading the news like a shiver

through bone. His mother
was no longer needed at the diner

across the river in Detroit. Foreigners
were worried back across the bridge

to Canada, were she got sick.
No health care or insurance, but doctors

and hospitals needed payment. Father
had to cash his pension. A scheme

being a condition of employment, the job
on the Streetcar line was lost.

They put the house up. Mother
read her brother's wire from England,

"Loads of work back 'ome 'ere, he says."
Across the sea, they wove, one

of a band of smoking hulks rising
and diving into the grey foam,

the Steward feeding him ice cream
every evening meal. "Keep 'em 'appy."

he said. And something about
"'Opin' Jerry don't loight up the noight."

The new Headmaster wasn't so
cheerful with his working class

farm labourers, least needing a
"colonial foisted 'pon themall."

(B)RUSH STROKE

1940: Invaded countries outnumber those on rations, for now; Graham Greene publishes The Power and the Glory, *Eugene O'Neill,* Long Day's Journey into Night, *George Santayana* The Realms of Being; *London is Blitzed; Jews are rounded up; penicillin becomes practical*

The red paint
which used to make the bicycle go

dries in a smeared pool
on the pavement.

The wheels have stopped
turning

but are round and full
in the sunshine

where the punctured spray can
was kicked about

and dragged away
by uniformed boys.

A RESTORATION FABLE

1941: U.S. Ambassador Joseph Grew warns of Japanese attack; Virginia Wolfe walks into a river; How Green Was My Valley *fills theatres; Pearl Harbour becomes a theatre for war; Intrepid convinces President Roosevelt that Wild Bill Donovan start up the OSS, later, the CIA*

When the dam broke
    it seemed rain
remembered its claim
to an ancient lake.

Flood-waters planed
over fences and roads.

Doors were pried open   windows
pulled from their sockets.

A human chain was formed to   reach
the school;
pass the children
across the swift running road.
Arm to arm,
baptism of mayhem.

Until,
the storm cleared into night
and light-beams from boats
swept along the channelled homes.

Oars   banged roofs.
Men   waited not to cry
when a bed of stuffed toys floated by

and a cow, four legs up, swirled
in the slow, shimmering reflection
over the moon.

She called for her children in the dark.

MARGERY

1942: Canada interns Japanese/Canadians into concentration camps; Britain introduces the wartime National Loaf; Books: Enrich Fromm The Fear of Freedom, *William Rose Benet* The Dust Which is God; Bambi *fills the screen in North American theatres*

Cleans the house
she grew up in,

sorts hand-me-downs,
treasures, and junk
into vegetable

crates. Finds
blue memories in a cracked dish
at the back of the wooden cupboard,
or, frozen faces
trapped in the grey ice of stained photos
in the damp corner
of the basement.

No one smiles in the pictures, but the faces
are familiar. She senses them later,
watching over her
as she kneels to pull overgrown irises from the side garden,
shakes the roots in the sky.

Beyond the wire fence,
a lone maple stands
in the blowing grass,
where a slim line of broken white stones
slant against the horizon.

Her hands push down on her thighs
through derelict wheat
to moss slates,
where the script

has been worn-off by crickets
singing her name.

DESIGN

1943: U.S. planes sink 22 Japanese ships; Allies begin round-the-clock bombing of Germany; in the Arts: William Saroyan The Human Comedy, Henry Moore Madonna and Child, Casablanca, Comin' in on a Wing and a Prayer, *the Zoot suit, the jitterbug*

Alicia loved the chess
of baseball's changing pitchers
mid-inning, wind-up sinker, by you too *fast*
fastball, and unpredictable
knuckleball wandering
the strike zone. She loved
sketching players in their
butt-tight uniforms, too. Charcoal
smooth as the arc of a line drive
up the middle. The crowd singing, swaying.
"Hey, hey, go-od bye."

Hot dogs, pizza, beer,
huddled lovers under park lights
taller than the church spire
and smoke stack
at the car plant. Her desk
on a curve of the horizon over
looking the parking lot
and stadium toward town hall
with its propensity for deals
that favoured drink
at functions where rook rules
were shadowed by knights,
cornered by corporate bishops,
slain by a silent Queen.

Third base made a sprawling dive,
she darkened the lines of her
pawn. The mayor and his politics,
what a winsome catch
his boy would make.

A PARISH SWAN

1944: Joyce Cary publishes The Horse's Mouth, *John Hilton* Rich Man, Poor Man; *Paul Klee's work is exhibited at Art Concrete; D-day begins; 1st non-stop flight from London to Canada; V-1 rockets drop on London*

Cygnets swam in order
along the ice line
where grey current flowed
under white sheets
of river through the village
on this quiet Sunday,
church bells tolling

down sheltered,
sided streets;
Yseult's breath
a tome of frost
for their craned necks
trumpeting her brothers'
choice of partner; the cold snap

having turned her collar
against weightless, swirling snow
lifted back to cloud as if
ice could fly,
or was afraid of warm
soft ground, damp
with previous melt, a water table

so high this year, fields
become a requiem
of earth, air and moisture
that frocked choir boys cried about
in paneled basement halls,
while the Parish swan preened
before taking flight.

REFRIGERATION CLASS

1945: Hitler commits suicide, U.S. drops atomic bomb on Japan; George Orwell publishes Animal Farm; *George Patton dies in a car; Soviet embassy clerk Igor Gouzenko astounded by Canadian liberties defects in Ottawa; a plane slams the Empire State building*

The plaid, buttoned-up
teacher said, "You can't
make something cold, you
can only take away its heat."

But what is it
about flame
leaned away
from the wick.

A freezer's breath, the cool
chill of a swamp, fog
drawn across a road.

The sun must have flickered
through the trees, a moth
fluttered in a gust of wind

the brief silence after a crash.

BARBED WIRE AND WILD ROSES

1946: New York becomes UN headquarters; spy rings collapse in Canada, Britain and U.S.; politicians, nuclear scientists, the Rosenbergs fall in a depth of spying never seen before — Russia was an Ally; Graham Sutherland paints Head of Thorns; *the Cold War begins*

Sex was a word they were not
allowed to say, their parents holding it

aloft when the boys played
hide'n'seek with homework due, frogs

singing in late spring, train whistles
narrowing the landscape.

On a clear fine day Cole
and Jesse ducked over the fence

of a dead end street, crossed the tracks,
and farmer's field to the cow pond. Cole

had a magazine from his Dad's
dresser. They sat against a post, barbed

wire laced with wild pink roses, and studied
a landscape of mushrooms and flowers.

But Jesse's sister had followed with a friend.
"Like a bad cold." Jesse wiped his nose

on his sleeve and hid the book. They sank stones
in the murky water, until Donna screamed,

"Look what they got." She and Jesse
went swimming. Cole and Susie followed.

In the noon sun, they played truth or dare
in the stubble wheat.

JERRY

1950: China occupies Tibet; N. Korea captures Seoul; U.S. supplies Saigon with arms; All about Eve *wins the Oscar; 1.5 million TV sets in America will become 15 million within a year; Robert Penn Warren writes* World Enough and Time, *Sartre* Troubled Sleep

Jerry broke shale
for luxury car mufflers;
the jagged scree
shovelled into buckets,
chain-hoisted to a cross-beamed ceiling,
and dumped
into a Y'd open chute.

The melted rock poured
from the furnace spout, bright lava
on a spinning wheel –
galaxied across darkness

into a vacuum of spun-stone
filling a sealed room,
pitch-forked (unmasked)
into bags, weighed, stacked
and shipped beyond midnight

but for the tiny
spines of glass-shards rising
inverted rain floating through the glare
of the rail dock lights.

Jerry butted his cigarette
tried not to brush his arm
against anything, less
the needles that covered his clothes,
were driven further
into his pores.
He coughed heavily, spat
up a spindly oyster.
The hard wrinkles
of his drawn face
settled in shadow —
eyes of salt-ale,
and a throat parched
for last call.

SOLDIER'S HEART

1951: N. Korea takes Seoul; 700 Canadian volunteers hold Hill 677 (gateway to Saigon) against 5000 Chinese; of the Canadian survivors, WWII vets, many will die as drunks; J.D. Salinger publishes Catcher in the Rye; *Bogey and Katherine Hepburn star in* The African Queen

Jill liked puzzles.
Words, numbers, anything
that would fill the calendar
each and every cleaning of the washroom,
laundry, breakfast-lunch-dinner,
while Jack brushed through his comic books

in the den. At least, he slept there now,
in that room. She didn't have to carry him
anymore. Didn't have to sleep with the
kicking, tossing, shouting, trying
to out-run the fires that crushed him.

By mid-noon, most days, he'd strap himself
into his wire wheels and fly
down the front ramp, up the drive, glide
along the walk to the park
where the kids soared
on their wheeled boards.

Until they'd tire of his haunted eyes
and snake away along the walk.
Head down. Jack would churn home. Up
the plywood ramp, back-arm
the door, bump his piece-
a-crap-chair over the sill, re-scar
the marred walls and twist
against the effin' table where her cracked
and re-glued china
figurines would be re-sent
                into tragic flight.

In the sunny parlour with her cross-
words, Jill would sigh. The broom
and dust pan
were in the cupboard, glue
in the drawer by the telephone
in the hall.

TEEM

1952: August, 16,000 escape East Berlin; Samuel Beckett writes Waiting for Godot, *John Steinbeck* East of Eden, *Edna Ferber* Giant; *Protestants revise the Bible; in film:* High Noon *and* The Greatest Show on Earth; *in song* It Takes Two to Tango

We emerge from warm sand
with the knowledge of death tucked away

in our shells
as we head toward the sun, gulls

screeching of shadows
on the way to waves, the need

of diving under
offset by the need to surface, to breathe

in the blue walled depth
above sharks.

SMELTING

1953: Rosenbergs executed; Arthur Miller writes The Crucible, Simone de Beauvoir, The Second Sex; *Hillary and Tenzing climb Everest; Elizabeth II crowned; Frank Sinatra wins an Oscar for:* From Here to Eternity; *Stalin dies; Armistice between the Koreas begins*

Out back they tossed cigarettes
and lunch bags in opposite
directions, clearly marked
against the occasional fire, back

where the loading dock sparkles
with shimmering flecks
of aluminum
from the STAMP presses.

Davy thinks aluminum is bad
for you, but can't
remember why. Though,

he knows when it rains,
a shiny crystal river flows
out the ditch to the lake.

He asked the boss once
'bout it. Ole Heckly
sighed, scratched his head,

"Don't know," he said, glancing
at the passing clouds. "But, Hey!
Don't you have work to do?"

ARMED PEACE:
1954 TO PRESENT

Canada has participated in policing, medical, humanitarian, and disaster relief every year all over the world since 1954, and has the 2nd highest fatality rate for peacekeepers. Yet in 2006, the UN ranked them 55th for commitment.

> and he delivered the news to shore
> that we do not die
> always as angels
> no, some of us go to amuse the cruel gods
>
> John B. Lee

DARGMAR AND JORGE

1954-5: Polio vaccinations begin; McCarthy witchhunt ends; Ian Fleming publishes Live and Let Die; *Canada and U.S. build radar stations across the north to counter Russia's military build-up; Aaron Copeland's* The Tender Land *opens in New York*

Dargmar and Jorge shovel dirt
to make a hole.
They pile the hole in the middle

of the island. Some rolls back in.
They keep digging
through the strata-clay

until their crushed morning bounces
off the treasure-lid
of the wiring box. Dargmar

negotiates a tide of traffic ebbing
the intersection, and wades a far shore
of boulevard heat, while managers

conference the truck. The day
wending like stone;
the sunken slab of concrete

they chip, sledge
hammers stuttering:
two beers and a whiskey,
two beers and a whiskey.

HOW SOFT THE SNOW

1956-8: Peacekeeping Forces solve Suez Crises, Lester Pearson receives a Nobel for the idea; Around the World in Eighty Days *wins the Oscar; Avro's Arrow Interceptor breaks Mach speed records; Russia launches Sputnik; Elvis is the rage; Jack Kerouac publishes* On the Road

Each year the children's shoes
thumped a size bigger, their clothes
stretched to splitting, seed
casting off shells. Tatya

accepted this like she accepted
old clothes from strangers,
to patch, while Jas
gave away his carrots, beets, turnips
from their yard-wide garden.

Until the mill began to hire,
then, Jas got a job unloading
50 lb. bags from boxcars. He'd
arrive home, head to toe in silica,
his accent as thick as a down

quilt, greeting the children, patting
their heads with powder like flour.
"Na zdorov'ya, little ones," he'd say,
until he died. Tatya
carried on, somehow, teaching

the girls to sew, the boys to
learn trades. Until,
she died too,
from happiness they said,
singing with her daughters' daughters

in church. She's buried, now,
beside Jas under a stone
as wide as a wheat field
as deep as snow.

HANDFUL OF WIND

1960-3: U.S. spy plane shot down over Russia; Eichmann arrested; Cuban missile crisis crops up; it is a time of books: To Kill a Mockingbird, The Loneliness of the Long Distance Runner, A Man for All Seasons, Catch 22, Silent Spring; *riots permeate the south; President Kennedy is shot*

The old man's fingers
twine in the fence that encages
the compound.

He calls to the foreigners
filing past — those
who mutter doctrine,
of doctoring solutions —

and holds his grandchild,
a shrunken leather bag
in his arm,
against the linkage.

Sand whorls
where eyes should be,
threadbare clothes flail —
flag of a different god.

He squeezes his hand
through the diamond chain,
palm to sun
divining food,
water,
any answer to death.

They give him a book
and set of sticks, one tied
across the other

to start a fire
among his people.

TRIGGER

1964: Peace Keepers take a position between Greeks and Turks in Cyprus; Beatles release their film: A Hard Day's Night; *Marshall McLuhan discusses his* Understanding the Media; *U.S. sprays Vietnam jungle with Agent Orange*

Gwen followed Tony into the Happiness-
by-the-glass Bar. Their boots
heavy on the dance floor
as sound equipment snored
in the corner.

She did her best to keep her hand off the gun.
"Just know where it is," Tony had said in the car.
Quick glances from the patrons slid
across their uniforms, and bright badges.
Tony tilted his cap to the rising conversations,
wrapped an arm around the bartender.

They laughed like old buddies,
snooker balls clacking in the back room.
Tony parted the bead curtain, bursts
of cursive rock drilled their ears. Gwen
remembered to take her hand off the gun.

In the sparse smoke, a medium height, 180
pound, caucasian, male, goes by the name Jarred,
as in preserves,
mounted a table and thumped a white ball into an equation
of bumpers. A red fell. The pink crept
toward a side pocket.

This chained, leather-vested streak of scruff
chalked his cue and grinned at Gwen,
"Whadda we got here? A quick-shot
all lined up." He humped the table and dropped
the pink, the cue ball banking
the horns of the hole.
It stopped in front of another red.

A stick of blonde tattoo puckered herself across his shoulder.

Gwen's finger pulsed.

SUMMER OF 65

1965: Ontario relay malfunction blacks out entire N.E., population spikes nine months later; Canada officially out of Vietnam war, supplies American troops; 30,000 Canadians join U.S. forces; President Johnson grabs P.M. Pearson's lapels for "pissing on his carpet"; Ralph Nadar writes Unsafe At Any Speed

Coach spewed blood and guts, and foot-
ball was war, since he lost part
of something back in Nam. "CRUSH
your opponent!" He said, and lined up

across from a mop-top sub, and crushed
him into mud. "That is what it's about.
Boys!" His grey, bristled head glistened

with sweat. He pointed at a young, slit-eyed
foreigner, second string corner-back
of a limp-wrist hippie. "Next," Coach said,
and crushed the sod chewing punk

into earth. "Weak. Like this society.
Now, stand, again! Or, be crushed,
Hippie boy." Yan spat grass
through his mouth guard. "You got

no equipment." Coach ignored him
and crouched on all fours. Yan spread
his feet, cushioned his knees. At the wheel
of the whistle he locked his legs and drove

his fore-arm up-through Coach's face.
Mashed, bloodied, eyes bulging,
Coach rolled on the ground trying to see
"wha'tha'fuck" just happened. Yan

sparked his spikes across the asphalt. Threw
his helmet, jersey and pads on the bench
and pulled on his hall-clicking leathers
to slam a field of uprights.

ALWAYS, THERE ARE FLOWERS

1966-7: Canada turns 100; Britain comes to celebrate, France demands Quebec be freed, both refuse secession within their own borders; J. K. Galbraith publishes The New Industrial State; *Montreal hosts Expo;* Fahrenheit 451 *and* The Heat of the Night *are in theatres;* Born Free *&* Eleanor Rigby *rule the radio; The Band helps Dylan go Electric*

No one ever bothered Art,
except to flower him in curses
if he kept bumming smokes, or, water him
in smokey compliments if they needed
a bit of change to make tab, yelling
"Thanks, Buddy" into the poppy patch of skin
that used to be his ear
before a war ended war, which Art
never talked about,

    sitting quietly, chuntering
to himself as waiters wiped away
the foam and salt spilled rings
of his chequered table, their shadows passing
through the evening sun as it washed across
the television, the anchorman's story
rolling out like a spent wave. Art

    would stumble up the back stairs, fall
into the bed of his room, which was not
a beach in France, not the woven thorns
of European streets torn inside out, nor
was it the wild flower fields, dug down
to tumbled roots of shriveled bodies, no.
It was just bed sheets, stained and worn,
where the German flower girl with the dirty
blonde hair, and basket of silent
trumpets washed of colour, waited, not
by the barracks, nor the Dance Hall,
but at a place among the crushed buildings
of war where "das light cahn't be killt."

In his chair for last call, Art's hair
would be slicked back, and he'd have
too much aftershave on his stubbled face.
And he'd drink
slow and steady under the fake-beamed
ceiling of a reproduced English Manor
with dead rabbits on fine china, horns
of fruit, and bouquets of flowers covering
the walls.

HOME RENO

1968-9: Humans walk on the moon; Canada allows draft dodgers to stay; Martin Luther King and Bobby Kennedy are assassinated; USSR invades Czechs; 1st ATM opens; 1st Big Mac is served; the Doors Unknown Soldier *is banded; Woodstock rocks; the Manson gang murders*

The fragile head filled the crutch
of Jarred's tattooed arm.
He kissed the blank curve
of canvas above the brow
as the boy blew bubbles, and kicked
like a runner going nowhere.

The phone jingled.
A voice curred, "Reno job. Tonight.
Out of town. We got tools. Meet at…"
Jarred laid the baby in the crib,
moved the phone
to his other ear, knowing
such small device could record

a whisper to a shout.
"Weather's hot. I don't think
I can make it."
"You don't think! Fuckin'
right, you don't think…"

Tiny hands pawed
Jarred's thick, callused fist,
prying it open. New teeth

gnawed at his finger.
"Go to sleep."
The phone canned to silence.

"My kid.
I'm talking to my kid."

FAITH

1970-1: Pierre Laporte is murdered by Quebec terrorists; P.M. Trudeau sends in the army; at Kent State, soldiers kill students; Gerhard Hertzog wins Nobel for studying Smog; Canada officially adopts multiculturalism; Guess Who release American Woman, *Neil Young,* Ohio

The August party was underway
before the upcoming semester –
music blaring, guests sating
themselves on wine, cheese, and thin

slices of politics de jour
while Faith watched for Perseids soaring
over the wall of trees in the back yard.
Michael, catching the tail of another,

said they were "stones thrown by God
smiting the wicked." Faith laughed,
"Doesn't He have enough trouble already
with Abraham's children fighting

amongst themselves. Like,
what kind of father was the guy?"
But her words were washed away
in the cranked stereo slamming

the damp hummus of the garden.
A dog, behind a board fence, began hounding
a startled reveille that echoed the metal
of garage doors, and drummed

the hollow rows of brick homes. The pale
yard ignited. The neighbour stood,
on his back porch, hands
holstered to hips.

He shouted through
the music.
"How'bout some
Goddamn Peace'n'Quiet!"

OLD MY GUITAR

1972-5: Rosemary Brown, a black woman, is elected to Canadian parliament; Canada launches the 1st domestic communications satellite; Atari releases Pong; *Baryshnikov defects in Montreal; Saigon falls; Hoffa disappears;* Taking Care of Business *hits #1 in N.America*

The Strike was a broken fence of workers
chopping wood saying, "winter's here,"
their feet shuffling to the blazing barrel
dance as daylight dwindled into hot rusted
nails. Old man Martel, his face a mouldy
moon of company glass, threatened to hose
them off the property. Guy-Jean strummed a two
by four: "You play wit yours, I play wit mine.
We play alone to-GET-er." They charged

morning's gate as light broke over barren
trees, a murder of crows cursed their ever-
tightening circle. Martel inched his car
against their knees. Then left it
in the street, and two-stepped to the office.
A Cop arrived within minutes. Said, "How's it
going men!" Said, he'd straighten this mess
out. Their fellow-union-brother chasséd
the bottom step with Martel. "Move it,
boys!" His cruiser exhausted their crowd.
Guy-Jean pounded his chords: "You take
da high road, and You take da low road…"

Home-made hooch washed down
the streetlight pizza on a tin lid. Suzi Sun's warm
noodle soup. Yuri's stuffed peroghys. Nicolas's
dollops of olive dip and pitas. Olga's thick
bread and stew, dark as a feast, shortened the fact
money was running out. Guy-Jean plucked at
a smooth-necked broom: "Canned goods fer Xmas
go by wit da whimper. Dhese are not a few
of my favourite tings." Spring came. Homes

were lost. A few folk skipped out on debts. Others got jobs: some good, some not so. The Company offered less than what was rejected. The Union said 'Take it.' Guy-Jean strolled around the barrel with a shovel: "It's da long way to da Union hall. So, flush twice boys…fer me." The second week after they settled, day shift strolled by Martel's new Caddy parked affront of the mill. Guy-Jean handed someone his lunch pail, "'old my gha-tar."

DUTCHIE

1978-9: Israel invades Lebanon; Elvis is dead; Space Invader game is #1; 1st test tube baby born; Jim Jones demands mass suicide, whether God showed up or not is a contentious issue; Pennsylvania reactor melts; China instills one child law; Pink Floyd releases The Wall

Jake and Emily sat deadheading flowers
when old Wily, the furnace salesman,
crossed the street with his boxer-bulldog
barreling ahead like a toy tank in a spiked
collar wrapped with an American-flag.

Wily gleamed with news. "Hear Ole Deischman
bought it. Can't say I'll miss him." Emily
pushed the dog's face from her crotch.
"Not ole Dutchie?" She squinted at Wily's sharp
silhouette. Just-call-me-Dutchie had had

white hair that swirled like homemade cream
puffs he hand-delivered on his one-speed,
squeaky-pedal bike. Wily looked puzzled.
"Dutch? Try Nat-zi," he exclaimed
like a sneeze. "But, My Gawd, you folks

are naive, aren't you?" He gazed up the street,
trying not to laugh as the dog pissed on Emily's
prize winning hydrangea. "Told you
he was Dutch did he with that long, red-brick,
cook-house of a barbecue looks like a mini

Dachau in the back yard. And, I mean really,
that shed with the winged propeller like some squat,
out-of-proportion windmill?" The dog's claws
raked at the grass. Wily yanked its chain.
"Come on, Sherman, we got flyers to deliver."

I OF DEATH

1980's: walking a Saskatchewan wheat field, Gorbachev decides to end the Cold War; John Lennon is killed by a fictionally deluded man; AIDS surges; Iran takes U.S. hostages; DNA is profiled; Rainbow Warrior is sunk; Chernobyl melts; Tiananmen protesters are crushed; a 1/2 million Vietnam children have been born with birth defects since the 60's

Padmavati waited at the green
light as cars
moved slowly through the red.
Her long nails tapped the steering
wheel to the refrain
of Lennon's 'Imagine.'
Maddy
would be so furious
if Paddy were late.
A loud blast
bruised the air behind her.
A silver Caddy
veered into the blind lane, cut
in front of her,
spangling her grill with stones.
The mad-dashed
purple-fumed rage
severed the flagged procession,

a blade of sun sliced the world
in half.
The driver waved for Paddy
to go too, if she really needed to,
but Paddy
let go of the wheel and raised
her palms.
A child in the back seat stared.

SUSIE

1989-91: Lech Walesa meets Polish officials to discus democratic transition; IRA bombs mainland Britain; the Germanys unite; 14 women are killed for attending a Montreal engineering school; Fatwa issued for Salmon Rushdie; Tim Berners-Lee proposes a World Wide Web; Ozone depletion discovered

Little birds attacked,
filling the house with invisible fumes
that wasn't smoke
in their throats.

Mr. Reilly from next door,
clouds perched behind his eyes,
climbed a ladder, and pulled the tin cap
off the chimney.

He threw a big ball of grass
to the ground,
while the mother sparrow
dive-bombed his head,

and Susie, without her studs,
earrings or chains, screeched
at the little featherless chicks
needing to be saved.

She jumped up and down
waving her arms
at the broken, forlorn nest
with the roof ripped off

and them 'peeping'
like the alarm in the hall had beeped
and mom had yelled
for them to run with what they had on,

to stand
by the curb in cool April
with Mr. Reilly,
his arms crossed, watching them die.

RANDY

1992-3: Officers of the Law are caught on tape laying a beating to Rodney King; US agents storm Waco, Texas; the Pentium chip and Beanie Babies flood world markets; Canadian soldiers commit torture in Somalia; Unforgiven *wins the Oscar;* Tears in Heaven *a Grammy*

Arthur sat in front of the heater
in his plywood cabin as waves
of hot air wilted the calendar girl, his cold
fingers polishing the money-box smooth
under the counter.

His bounty of hidden remedies
on the scarred shelf didn't seem
to be working: Bombay gin, California
raisins, pineapple juice, dried
sour cherries, copper bracelet, magnets.
He looked at his watch, then cracked
open the window, "I don't pay you guys
to drink coffee." The pane, sparkled
by the worn-out flick of a florescent
light, dripped with condensation. The boys
shuffled back to their concrete pads, tossed
their cups on the ground. Ole Randy
looked up, "Yes Sir, Mr. Eitaz, sir,"
he exhaled cloud and yanked a ligament
of hose from a coiled compressor, broke
shards of plastic from air conditioners,
unwound wire from old transformers until
the edge of night settled under his skin.

At the hotel, he ripped the top off
his pay packet and sucked back
a few beers, while grumbling how stingy
Ole man Eitaz could be.
The Bar owner yelled over,
"Take yer coat off an stay awhile."
Old Randy said he couldn't stay.
Though he did,
leaning against the radiator
to ward off the bad surgeon with the dull knife
that worked his shoulder each
and every night.

THE BLUE CHARGER

1994-6: Mandela wins S.Africa Presidency; General Romeo Dallaire meets the devil; Oklahoma terrorists bomb the Feds; mad cow kills humans, most countries stop feeding beef to cows; The Stone Diaries *wins a Pulitzer; Jerry Garcia of the Grateful Dead dies; 1st animal cloned;* Jagged Little Pill *wins a Grammy*

David turned off his mobile
and weighted it in his jacket pocket.
He dumped two sugars and a swirl
of whitener into a squeaking
foam cup, and turned to Bryant,
"Cancer. Michael would'a'bin fifty."

They found small sandwiches on paper plates,
the bread starting to curl.
David steered clear of the egg-salad as Michael's
life spread out before them on bulletin boards.
The last pic was a lean young man leaned
against a chromed-out Blue Charger.
Bryant took a helping of potatoes. "Fast?"
he asked.

Direction is a strange highway
when your heart wills a car
around a 2am curve of tunneled
woodland. "Hospital," David had yelled
to the cop who had pulled them over,
his lights racing ahead only to
race past them again.

David grabbed the head-lolled
dead-weight-of-Michael from the dark-
pooled passenger side; a blood-tied
t-shirt wrapped around his beer-drinking-fist.
He layered him on a gurney, Michael
whiter than the sheet. The cop
asked what happened. David turned away,
"Fuck off."
The cop brought over
some really bad coffee, gave one
to David. David was quiet, then asked the cop if he knew
where the wind comes from in the morning when you're out
fishing and the lake just ruffles over
right as the sun comes up.

The cop said his name was Steve,
and that he didn't know. Then the doctor
walked in, said, sober as dawn, "He'll live."

Under the doctor's binocular gaze, and the cop's
inverted stance, David didn't say anything
about rifling cottages, or Michael grabbing his fist
like a drunk with the wrong set of keys, or that panic came
in a flashlight showing shards of glass
shining brighter than stars bleeding light
from Michael's veins. "He fell," David said.

With the wind cupped into his hand, Michael
held a cigarette as the Blue Charger purred
through the countryside awash with cool-reed-lakes
and sun-burst-trees, the light stinging their eyes
through the windshield. "Any beers left,"
Michael smiled, staring at his smokin' bandage.

Bryant's callused, mechanic's fingers
tumbled a square of dessert into his mouth,
crumbs fell as he asked, "So. What happened
to it? The car?" David's gaze settled on the long
haired boy in the picture. "It's up on blocks."

MS. N

1999-2000:Y2K: planes will fall from the sky; disgruntled gamers with guns kill at Columbine; Kevorkian guilty of voluntary euthanasia; the clock ticks on and the sky doesn't fall, experts melt into 'Chicken Little' history; investment scams flourish; thousands lose their jobs

Below the hill outside of town
is where the forge used to echo
off the low, moon-lit clouds on restless nights.
She remembered pressing her nose to the screen,
and listening to the strikes of the devil's heart
as crickets plucked
their grass harps in the bright
streetlight pools
as curious raccoons rattled shadows
in their tin neighbourhood
full of sheds and garages.
"What are you looking for?" She'd called down,
the raccoon's glassy eyes looking up
as the midnight train trundled
over the clacking trestle, carrying
factory wares south, bringing empty cars
home, the whistle smoking the fields
they used to run. Her and Joey,
'til he lost his leg under the shunting freight.

They'd been collecting blue iron balls
along the tracks. Her brother had said,
"The rail-line'll give ya a million bucks
if ya get a ton of 'em." Why Joey ever hopped
the moving train was beyond her.

They never got their million. Never
worked the forge, never
operated the hammer in the night.
All the little blue balls having rolled away.

The old factory's a call centre now,
car-parts made in Mexico where the bright homes
and gardens full of gnomes have gone. Though, crickets
still harp the shadows, and raccoons
still worry the night, until the express shoots by
in the morning taking the east folk west
and the west folk east.

NAN'S MOM

2001-3: disaffected Saudi rebels destroy the twin towers; New York reels under ash; airspace over N.America shuts down; towns in Canada become passenger cities needing food, shelter, water; some U.S. officials blame Canada's porous borders; pilots trained in U.S.; Blame it on Canada *popular U.S. cartoon; human genome project completed; SARS spreads*

Nan's mom picked up a box
of pre-cooked ribs, the picture on the side
sopping with sauce. "Dease weal good," she said,
her thin pearled hand dropping it into the cart
as rain pelted the store-length windows.
She scanned palm-down along the coloured shelves –
embroidered coat open, silk scarf
covering the wrinkled cross-patterned neck,
under her soft, white hair.

Over the phone, she'd said,
"Storm on way. I need fruit. Milk. You,
to carry in house."
Then, on the drive to the mall, "By way,
eye not take. Make me wonder 'bout getting
other done. Doc-tow say opa-Ation wen well.
Nu'se sink I allergic to eye-drop.
Only sing is waun stop lea-king. You know,
how bo-kan win-dow is. That how I see, now.
Fac-sured wain-bows."

Nan turned from the frozen trout's
shrunken eyes and fought the cart
toward the canned goods aisle.
Her mom laughed, "Wewl,
least I still see." She pointed to a jazzy
coloured jar of polka kraut with veg,
"Dis wweeaall good."
She slid the spiced cabbage into the cart. The glass
dented a package of frozen peas, glanced sideways
against the milk, releasing a flood of condensation.
Beyond the registers, the window streamed
with rain as a mother in the parking lot
loaded groceries into her car. The daughter,
beside the open trunk,
stood with her head tilted back, mouth wide open,
screaming at heaven.

GREG: CORP OF ENGINEERS, AFGHANISTAN

2004-6: Facebook and Twitter are darlings of the new age; piracy of personal information prospers like never before; terrorism begins to multiply exponentially; Saddam Hussein executed for Tyranny; N. Korea detonates a nuclear bomb; Crash *wins Oscar; Martha Stewart is jailed*

It was a mean
while, and fuckin' warm,

as we swarmed
a pact-racket of battle-hungry
rag-tag, mis-fits

when it all kettles
into sky.

~

Breath rattled,
I pulls Vincent through his tea

flak-jack torn, back
behind a mud clump wall

as bullets
holed the air.

MAEVE

2007:Canada uses clear/hold/build strategy to fix Southern Afghanistan; Benazir Bhutto is assassinated; Bush denies global warming; The Departed, *and* An Inconvenient Truth *win Oscars; a Grammy goes to* Not Ready to Make Nice; *Doris Lessing wins a Nobel*

Maeve pecked at dysentery, cholera,
while Netty hummed to the swollen
earthly bodies and moons
of children; smoke
rising from the dung and grass fires
of the thousands nestled on trampled fields.

Maeve didn't care that Netty called herself
Nurse
as long as she could do a decent bandage.

In the shimmering heat, a line of adults,
their ball cap hats like curved beaks,
circled among the dying. "A better place,"
Netty overheard, as a laying-on of hands
began, and a clutch of children grew longer.

"The world needs to know, mother."
Netty chirped as Maeve finished
the suture of a women's stump-leg
in the back of a pick-up truck,
Maeve's own shift feathered red.

The reporter sat outside the hotel,
scratching a few notes on his phone-pad
when a familiar woman hovered nearby.

Maeve stepped closer, flapping her hands
in front of her, trying to give flight to words
that wouldn't hatch, tears rolling
through the blood and dust of fear.

DWAYNE

2008-9: Barrack Obama wins the presidency; Canadian parliament prevents itself from functioning, prorogues; Canadians are on edge, hockey anthem is changed; Radovan Karadzic is extricated to the Hague; U.S. housing scheme brings down world banks; No Country for Old Men, Avatar & Slumdog Millionaire *reign at the box office*

Main Street's line of classics
gleamed, hood-raised above
chrome, orange, and lime green
blocks as ball-capped buffs
worried about clouds in the east.

Heads turned at each
polished fender: 49 Hudson,
57 Belair, 69 Cuda, 81 Bronco,
08 Civic...a Honda!

The foreigner slow paraded up Main
thumping passed Homestead Hardware
where Roger's Roadster sat angled
to the curb belting out the best
of the Beatles between a red Corvette
and a yellow Corvair.

Roger turned to Dwayne,
"Who the fuck let the rapper
in?" Dwayne pulled himself
out of his canvas chair beside the table
full of nodding bobble-heads
and jumped into his 73 camouflaged
RoadRunner and rumbled up
the ole V8, strafing the beige Civic
with red-line revolutions as lightning
raced the crowd for cover.

TO SAIL GRACEFULLY

2010-11: last Canadian WW1 vet dies, as does Steve Jobs; Bin Laden, Gadhafi are assassinated; no one is charged with fraud regarding world economic collapse; Gulf of Texas drowns in oil; Toronto G20 summit turns violent; abuse in retirement homes rises; Harvard kindles hope for living longer; a Prince marries a Princess, the world swoons

You talk clouds
from a tossed ocean
of hospital where you
curl forward, rain
ready to be reborn.

Blue is a reason, you sob,
folding pieces of light in toilet
paper: a pen, a few coins, a lost
credit card, we find furled under
green, riffled sheets "for the storm."

A spate of darkness you blame
on stale rations, lifeless air,
and distant lightning nurses
with electric pills that assail
you into this forlorn

state, your jib nosed
in a downdraft trough of self-
pity, rather than the getting up of
being dressed, all sails tact north-
west of salient form.

DEMO

2012: Mayan Calendar predicts an end; new migrants struggle between scripture and what is rule of law, one person retorts, 'You voted with your feet like the rest of us who come here.'; guns kill children in a Sandy Hook school; more Americans have been killed by their own guns, than all their foreign wars combined

He was always there
Wednesday nights just
before closing. Walked
10k to and from his house
on the escarpment. Liked

whatever was new. Never
bought anything.
His haversack drawn
tight to his hip, pursed
lip and flap combed over,
shut. A battered
ground lieutenant

in a field of product,
gait uneven
for the slow charge
across broken farmland
with twilight breaking. At the end
of the aisle-hedge, he carefully
examined a gunners pit

of tool display. Felt
the pistol-grip-drill fit
tight in his hand, laid it
back down marvelling
at the smallness of battery needed
to drive a screw

through a body of wood. A child
grabbed the gun and delighted
the trigger, holding it with two hands
the bit digging into the four
by four peppered with scars of used
and reused screws. "Cool,"

he said, skipping away. "It'll keep
driving," said an associate
over the lieutenant's shoulder, "until
you're clean through to the other side,"
her bright uniform the colour
of the framework shelves.

OVER THE FIELD, A LARK FLUTTERS - REMEMBERANCE DAY

2013: Edward Snowden reveals Canada as espionage power; unmarked fracking oil burns 49 people to death in Lac Megantic explosion; Tar Sand pipeline stalled for being dirty; Mandela passes; Alice Munro wins a Nobel; corrupt politicians make the news, if writers tell stories, what do politicians tell; comic heroes control the box office

She was up a way, staring
toward the crest of a hill

one arm pointing

a stiff
conductor. As I drew closer, her arms
were crossed
over her heart as if nursing a memory that could rip
her apart. There was
no bench to sit on, and frost covered the
path. Her long
coat, muddied, reminded me of a homeless
person, or entrenched
war vet trying to escape a de-forested past
or retrieve
a moment's notice of leaves, of memory
orchestrated,
falling from a bright yellow
maple. No one
was with her. I stood and watched
awhile, the cold
ticking off furled churning chutes into
the breeze
whirling down the field's fall-thrashed edge
splashed with red, only
to be trapped in the tomb-stalks of weeds, their
helmets fraught
with that thought-filled angle of spilling seed.

"Is everything okay," I asked.

"Was it a lark? Did you see?
I'm sure it was a lark."

2014: Canadian troops quietly leave Afghanistan; Europe vies for Ukraine, Russia storms Crimea, sanctions fly like pre-WW1 threats; internet fears continue to advise the refusal of inoculations; measles and other old diseases begin to reappear

War

ACKNOWLEDGEMENTS:

A great thank you to the teachers, editors and Wednesday poets who made me think and rethink, to my family because I don't stand alone, to the OAC, who assisted in the research of this project through a Writers' Reserve grant, and to Black Moss Press for being there.

ABOUT THE AUTHOR:

Keith is a multi-award winning poet whose work can be found in major journals across Canada, and in Ireland. To date, he has published two chapbooks: *Tactile Hunters*, Cubicle Press (2005) and *A Stone with Sails*, part of Sigilate Press's trilogy of Niagara Poets: *Hanging on a Nail* (2009). Keith lives in Thorold, Ontario.